Animals
of the
Past

by Beverley Dietz

 HOUGHTON MIFFLIN   BOSTON

Ichthyosaurus

Many kinds of animals are extinct. They lived on Earth at one time. Then they all died out.

Why did they become extinct? Sometimes their habitats changed. The animals did not have a good place to live. They did not have enough to eat. Sometimes the animals were hunted. So many were killed that the animals became extinct.

Compsognathus dinosaur

Long ago, many kinds of dinosaurs lived on Earth. Some were huge. Others were small. Some dinosaurs ate meat. Others ate only plants.

The last dinosaurs died about 65 million years ago.

Humans did not live on Earth at this time. No one is sure why dinosaurs became extinct.

Clam

Many kinds of animals have become extinct. This big clam is extinct now. The last ones died more than 30 million years ago.

Other kinds of clams still live in the seas. Some of them are in danger of becoming extinct too.

Sabre-tooth cat

These animals lived millions of years after the dinosaurs. They became extinct about 10,000 years ago.

These animals lived in the last Ice Age. Then the weather changed. The animals did not have a good place to live anymore.

Dodo

Dodo birds once lived on an island in the Indian Ocean. Then sailors came to the island. They cut down the forest where the dodos lived. The sailors ate dodos. They brought other animals, like cats, pigs, and rats. Those animals ate dodo eggs. They ate dodo chicks too. About 350 years ago, the dodo became extinct.

Passenger pigeon

Billions of these birds once flew in the air. Then people began to kill the birds. They wanted the birds for food. Now these birds are gone. The last one died about 100 years ago.

Giant panda

Many kinds of animals are endangered. Some are hunted. Others are losing their habitats. These animals need to be protected. Otherwise, they will become extinct.